I0540508

The Contemporary Board Member *is a must-read for today's Directors, offering guidance on leading with deliberation, fluency, range, and confidence. The book addresses how digital disruption, workforce transformation, and stakeholder activism challenge Boards in modern governance. Tom Mawhinney presents an adaptable approach to enhancing board effectiveness through self-assessment of leadership skills in Professional, Personal, and Technology areas, focusing on key skills needed now and in the future. I look forward to sharing this valuable resource with my Boards.*

BARBARA BOYD, CPA, CA, ICD.D – Independent Director,
Steam Whistle Brewing; Oshawa Power

Energizing ... The Contemporary Board Member *offers a new perspective on the accountability for individual board members to take charge of their continued development and to broaden their skills and competencies. Showing up is no longer acceptable. A powerful message to Board Chairs as well. Tom Mawhinney provides a good reminder that traditional lanes are no longer adequate coverage – the world is changing at a rapid pace and Board members need to understand how that applies and impacts their roles.*

RICHARD BOYER - Corporate Director - Triumph Real Estate
Investment Fund

THE
CONTEMPORARY
BOARD MEMBER

THE
CONTEMPORARY
BOARD MEMBER

The 15 Essential Leadership Skills
Re-imagined for the Modern Boardroom

TOM MAWHINNEY

THIN LEAF PRESS

The Contemporary Board Member. Copyright © 2025 by Tom Mawhinney. All rights reserved. No part of this publication may be reproduced, distributed, or transmitted in any form or by any means, including photocopying, recording, or other electronic or mechanical methods, without the prior written permission of the author, except in the case of brief quotations embodied in reviews and certain other non-commercial uses permitted by copyright law. The contributing authors maintain all rights to use the material inside the chapter he or she wrote for this book.

Disclaimer—The advice, guidelines, and all suggested material in this book are given in the spirit of information with no claims to any particular guaranteed outcomes. This book does not replace professional consultation. The author, publisher, editors, and organizers do not assume and hereby disclaim any liability to any party for any loss, damage, or disruption caused by anything written in this book.

Publication Data
Names: Mawhinney, Tom, Author
The Contemporary Board Member

ISBN: 978-1-953183-93-4 (paperback) | 978-1-953183-92-7 (eBook)

Business, Money, Management, Leadership
Editor: Dhanliza Cellona
Thin Leaf Press
Los Angeles

Book Cover Design by 100Covers.
Interior Formatting by Dindo B. Sanguenza.

THIN
LEAF

TABLE OF CONTENTS

INTRODUCTION

Board leadership today demands more—and allows no room for complacency. In a landscape shaped by complexity, scrutiny, and rapidly shifting stakeholder expectations, directors are no longer measured solely by what they oversee but by how they engage in the process. Presence matters. So does tone. So does the ability to hold space for difficult conversations without defaulting to deference or control. The modern board member doesn't just provide oversight— they shape how the organization navigates ambiguity. And there are fewer places to hide when that leadership falls short.

But the challenge isn't just the speed of change—it's the spread of it. Strategy is no longer separate from culture. Oversight can't be isolated to financials and fiduciary duties. Risk now includes platform, reputation, cybersecurity, stakeholder trust, and ethical decision making. Today's board members must navigate across unfamiliar terrain while holding their seat with clarity and restraint. That means asking sharper questions. Naming what's missing. And knowing when influence—not authority—is what leadership requires most.

In this world, governance is no longer a technical exercise. It's a leadership act. The most effective board members don't just bring experience. They bring capability—built deliberately, demonstrated under pressure, and continuously adapted to fit the realities of the organizations they serve. That's why this book exists. *The Contemporary Board Member* is a skills-based roadmap for modern governance leadership. It offers not just insight but also a clear path for strengthening how you contribute, challenge, and lead inside the boardroom—when the stakes are high and the script is rarely clear.

1

A Series Built for Context

This book is part of *The Contemporary Leader* series—a body of work designed to modernize leadership at every level of the enterprise. The series began with *The Contemporary Leader*, which introduced a foundational model: 15 essential leadership skills, organized across three core domains—professional, personal, and technology. These skills are the raw material of leadership in today's world. But how they're applied—and which ones matter most—depends entirely on the role you're in.

That's why this series doesn't stop at a universal framework. It scales across context. Each companion volume explores how the same leadership model must adapt to different seats. *The Contemporary Executive* examines how operating leaders show up with fluency and credibility in high-complexity environments. *The Contemporary Entrepreneur* explores how founders lead in motion, often under pressure and without structure. This book turns to the boardroom, where directors are expected to lead through oversight, inquiry, and long-term stewardship—often without the benefit of day-to-day context or organizational control.

In this environment, board members can't rely on instinct alone. They must develop a leadership skill set that's as clear and current as the challenges they're being asked to weigh in on. Governance is no longer a technical conversation. It's a leadership moment. And this book is here to help directors meet that moment with more fluency, more range, and more confidence in how they lead.

Why a Leadership Guide for Board Members?

Because modern governance isn't static—and most board development tools still treat it like it is. For decades, directors were expected to bring judgment, experience, and a steady hand. That hasn't changed. But what has changed is the range of issues boards are now expected to engage with—and the pace at which they're expected to weigh in.

It's not just oversight anymore. It's oversight with fluency. With range. With the ability to challenge constructively across strategy, culture, risk, digital transformation, stakeholder priorities, and more. The conversations around the board table have grown more complex. The expectations around director contribution have grown more specific. And the margin for showing up under prepared has narrowed.

Boardrooms used to allow for uneven leadership contributions. If you brought functional depth or committee experience, you could stay in your lane. But governance today is a shared seat. Strategy, talent, and ESG aren't just management concerns—they're board-level responsibilities. And that means every director must build the leadership fluency to engage across unfamiliar terrain without defaulting to deference, silence, or overreach.

This book doesn't suggest that board members need to act like executives or take over management's job. But it does challenge the idea that governance can remain a passive function. Because the boards that are most effective today aren't just diverse in composition—they're diverse in capability. Directors who take ownership of their leadership development aren't just contributing more—they're raising the standard for what board leadership looks like in a modern organization.

From Skills to Competencies to Governance Readiness

The 15 essential leadership skills introduced in *The Contemporary Leader* remain the foundation of this book—and the foundation of the series as a whole. They represent the raw material of modern leadership. But in the boardroom, effectiveness doesn't come from mastering individual skills in isolation. It comes from knowing how to apply them—together, in real time, under pressure.

That's where competencies come in.

A competency is more than a skill. It's what happens when multiple capabilities converge—applied with judgment, adapted to context, and used with fluency across the table. When communication, emotional intelligence, and decision making show up in a high-stakes CEO discussion, that's a competency. When technology objectivity, strategic visioning, and stakeholder awareness come together during a conversation about platform risk, that's a competency too.

These moments don't arrive neatly. They don't ask for one skill at a time. They come layered, compressed, and often without perfect information. And in the boardroom, where directors don't have day-to-day control or full visibility, the ability to integrate skills into real-time governance impact is what separates presence from performance.

That's why this book goes beyond naming the skills. It's about helping you apply them—in combinations that matter, at moments when leadership can't be delegated. Because at this level, board readiness isn't just about what you know. It's about how you lead when the conversation gets real.

Introducing David Chen

These concepts aren't just frameworks—they reflect the lived reality of boardroom leadership today: influence without authority, stakes without structure, and decisions that carry long-term consequence without perfect information. To make those ideas tangible, this book follows the evolving story of David Chen, a tenured director navigating a boardroom that no longer responds to experience alone.

David isn't new to governance. He's served on public and private boards across industries. He's respected by his peers and trusted by management. But as expectations evolve—faster decisions, sharper scrutiny, and more visibility—he begins to notice the signs. Discussions feel different. The issues are more layered. The tone around the board table has shifted. And while nothing is broken, the clarity he once brought now feels just slightly out of step.

David's not in crisis. But he's at a crossroads. And like many modern board members, he begins to realize that staying relevant requires more than showing up prepared. It requires building new fluency—across technology, tone, stakeholder dynamics, and governance leadership itself.

His story unfolds across each chapter, not as a perfect arc, but as a reflection of what board-level growth really looks like. His journey is specific, but the pressure is familiar. Because today, every director has to confront the same question: Is your leadership keeping pace with the boardroom you're sitting in?

What You'll Find in This Book

This book offers a structured approach to leadership development at the board level. It is designed to help directors identify the most relevant leadership skills for their role, prioritize where to grow, and apply those capabilities in ways that strengthen governance impact.

- *Chapter 1—The Contemporary Leader: A Foundation for Board Leadership*

  Reintroduces the leadership framework from *The Contemporary Leader*, with a focus on the three core domains—professional, personal, and technology— and how they apply in a governance context.

- *Chapter 2—The Evolving Role of Today's Board Member*

  Explores how governance expectations have expanded and why board members must now lead through influence, adaptability, and cross-functional awareness.

- *Chapter 3—Identifying and Prioritizing the Essential Boardroom Leadership Skills*

Helps directors determine which of the 15 leadership skills to focus on, based on their board role, organizational context, and long-term leadership goals.

- *Chapter 4—From Awareness to Action: Developing Essential Boardroom Leadership Skills*

  Outlines practical strategies—self-directed learning, peer engagement, structured education, and expert coaching—that directors can use to build relevant competencies over time.

These chapters are designed to work together—moving from foundational understanding to skill prioritization to real-world development. Whether you're a first-time director or a seasoned board chair, this book provides a clear and practical roadmap for becoming a more intentional and impactful leader in the boardroom.

My Experience with Governance Leadership

My perspective on board leadership comes from direct experience. Over the past two decades, I've served on multiple boards—including as committee chair, board chair, and independent director—across sectors, stages, and governance models. I've seen firsthand how boards operate when leadership is strong—and where they stall when it's not. I've also seen how much weight the individual director can carry, even when influence is quiet and authority is shared.

My formal training through the ICD.D designation deepened what I had already learned in practice: that governance effectiveness isn't just about process or oversight. It's about tone. Inquiry. The quality of presence a director brings when the room is split or the signal is unclear. And those aren't qualities that develop through experience alone. They have to be built deliberately.

This book reflects that belief. It's not about perfection. It's about posture. How we show up. How we grow. And how we lead when the boardroom stops being theoretical—and becomes the place where real influence lives.

A Final Note Before We Begin

Board service doesn't come with a manual—but it does come with weight. The decisions made in the boardroom shape more than strategy. They shape outcomes, reputations, and, increasingly, the public narrative around how an organization shows up in the world. In that environment, leadership at the board level isn't just about what you know. It's about how you engage.

This book isn't about becoming a different kind of director. It's about becoming a more deliberate one. The kind who leads with clarity, adapts with intention, and contributes in ways that reflect both experience and evolution. Because staying credible in the boardroom isn't about staying current on issues alone. It's about staying sharp in how you lead through them.

The work ahead is yours to do. This book is here to help you do it—strategically, credibly, and in rhythm with the organizations you serve.

CHAPTER 1

THE CONTEMPORARY LEADER - A FOUNDATION FOR BOARD LEADERSHIP

The expectations placed on today's board members have expanded far beyond traditional oversight. As governance becomes more complex and multidimensional, directors must draw from a broader set of leadership capabilities—ones that enable them to navigate emerging pressures with clarity, fluency, and perspective. This chapter reintroduces the leadership framework at the heart of *The Contemporary Leader* and sets the stage for how it will be applied throughout this book—specifically, in the context of boardroom leadership.

That framework is built around 15 essential leadership skills, organized into three domains: *professional*, *personal*, and *technology*. These skills form the foundation for leadership effectiveness across all levels—but their true value emerges when they are developed and applied in concert. For directors, that integration enables stronger contributions across every aspect of board service, from strategic inquiry and oversight to stakeholder engagement and long-term stewardship.

The Contemporary Board Member builds on this foundation with a focused lens. Board members do not lead through operational control—they lead through influence, inquiry, and perspective. To do so effectively, they must prioritize the capabilities that elevate their impact at the board level. By developing leadership range across all three domains, directors strengthen their ability to meet the full spectrum of modern governance demands—from regulatory shifts and economic volatility to digital transformation, talent dynamics, and stakeholder pressure. This book is not a restatement of previous ideas—it is a focused evolution, purpose-built for the boardroom and grounded in the realities of contemporary oversight.

The Evolving Business Landscape and the Need for Leadership Evolution

Board leadership today isn't defined by traditional oversight anymore. Directors are now positioned at the intersection of strategy, culture, technology, and stakeholder dynamics—where change doesn't wait for process to catch up. Governance expectations have evolved from structured review to active engagement, from committee specialization to enterprise fluency. Experience still matters. But how that experience is applied matters even more.

The pace of disruption isn't isolated to industries anymore—it reshapes governance itself. Strategic shifts emerge faster than board calendars. Talent and cultural challenges escalate in parallel with regulatory pressures. Technological developments—from AI adoption to cybersecurity risks—reach the board table before frameworks fully exist to manage them. Directors can no longer treat leadership as a secondary layer beneath fiduciary duties. It must be integrated into how they inquire, challenge, and guide organizations in motion.

This shift reframes the role of board members. It's no longer about arriving at the table with the right background. It's about staying credible across dimensions that no longer operate sequentially. Effective directors lead through convergence—where strategic oversight, ethical discernment, digital fluency, and cultural stewardship intersect at once. Leadership readiness in the boardroom now demands a different kind of skill set: practiced, integrated, and actively applied under conditions of accelerating complexity.

That's why this book builds on the leadership framework introduced in *The Contemporary Leader*. Not to restate familiar skills—but to help directors engage them differently: in ways that match the demands of governance today. Influence without authority, accountability without control, strategic clarity without perfect information—these aren't side challenges anymore. They are the seat itself. And the directors who lead fluently across them are the ones who raise the effectiveness—and resilience—of the boards they serve.

The Three Leadership Skill Domains: A Comprehensive Framework

The leadership model explored in *The Contemporary Leader* is structured around three domains: *professional*, *personal*, and *technology* skills. These domains serve as the foundation for effective leadership across roles—but in the context of the boardroom, their application takes on a distinct shape. Directors must draw from each domain with intention, integrating these capabilities to guide oversight, navigate complexity, and steward long-term value.

Within each domain sits a defined set of essential skills—15 in total. These are:

1. Professional Skills: Building a Foundation for Strategic Oversight

These six skills form the foundation of strategic boardroom contribution—enabling directors to engage complex issues with clarity, perspective, and credibility.

1. *Visioning* — crafting and sustaining a compelling long-term direction

2. *Translation* — converting strategy into clear, actionable steps

3. *Problem Solving* — navigating complex challenges with structure and creativity

4. *Decision Making* — evaluating risks and opportunities to make timely, informed choices

5. *Communication* — sharing ideas clearly, credibly, and with the right audience

6. *Motivation* — energizing others around purpose, progress, and possibility

Professional skills are not about managing execution—they are about enabling strategic influence. These skills allow directors to engage with complex issues, challenge assumptions, and support decision making through insight and perspective. They are also essential to one of the board's most under-leveraged contributions: translation. In a governance context, translation refers to the ability to connect abstract strategy to actionable priorities and to ensure that operational realities remain aligned with long-term intent.

While many directors bring deep executive experience, that experience does not automatically translate into effective boardroom contribution. The six *professional* skills must be applied with intention. They are not static capabilities; they evolve with context, and they must be revisited as the demands of governance change.

Directors should not assume mastery simply because they have practiced these skills in other settings. In fact, many of the most seasoned leaders overlook or underinvest in them when they step into governance roles. This section encourages a more deliberate approach—helping directors assess their current range, identify areas of strength or complacency, and target development efforts accordingly.

2. Personal Skills: Strengthening Boardroom Influence

These six skills form the foundation of boardroom influence—enabling directors to lead through complexity with trust, empathy, and presence.

1. *Coaching* — helping others grow by offering support, challenge, and feedback

2. *Authenticity* — leading with clarity, consistency, and a strong sense of self

3. Emotional Intelligence — understanding and managing emotions—your own and others'

4. *Curiosity* — pursuing new ideas and perspectives with openness and intention

5. *Adaptability* — adjusting quickly and effectively in response to change

6. *Resilience* — maintaining perspective and energy through adversity and uncertainty

Personal skills enable directors to lead through influence, not authority. In the boardroom, directors rarely exercise control, but they are expected to shape high-stakes decisions, foster trust across diverse stakeholders, and model composure under pressure. The ability to guide discussion, align perspectives, and bring forward both challenge and support requires a distinct form of leadership—one rooted in personal fluency and relational depth.

These capabilities help directors navigate interpersonal dynamics, build credibility with executives and peers, and respond thoughtfully to unexpected developments. They are especially important when oversight touches on issues like culture, succession, stakeholder engagement, or values-based decision making—areas where trust matters as much as expertise.

Boardroom success requires directors to apply *personal* skills with intention. Tenure or confidence does not automatically translate into relational leadership. This section encourages board members to reflect on how they show up in moments of dialogue, dissent, and disruption—and to strengthen the skills that allow them to lead with consistency, humility, and impact.

3. Technology Skills: Governing in a Digital World

These three skills form the foundation of digital oversight—ensuring that governance remains relevant, informed, and capable in a tech-driven landscape.

1. *Technology Awareness* — staying informed on emerging tools and trends

2. *Technology Objectivity* — assessing tech solutions with curiosity and discipline

3. *Technology Application* — using digital capabilities to create business value

Technology skills are now fundamental to boardroom credibility. Directors must be prepared to engage with digital disruption, AI ethics, cybersecurity, enterprise platforms, and data governance—often all at once. These issues are no longer technical edge cases; they are core to strategy, risk, and transformation.

The three *technology* skills—awareness, objectivity, and application—equip directors to ask sharper questions, evaluate risks with greater confidence, and shape technology strategy that delivers actual value. These are not about technical depth—they are about informed, contextual fluency.

Too often, directors defer to others when technology is discussed. But as digital capability becomes embedded in every strategic decision, governance requires more than passive awareness. This section challenges directors to develop these skills with intention—and to ensure the board's collective fluency evolves in step with the organizations they oversee.

Leadership at the board level isn't about mastering one domain in isolation. It's about navigating all three simultaneously— especially when expectations accelerate faster than board rhythms traditionally allow. These domains are interdependent, and their value compounds when they are applied in context. This framework exists to help directors lead with more clarity, more confidence, and more contribution.

For readers who want to explore each skill in greater depth, *The Contemporary Leader* provides a detailed reference that can be revisited in parallel with this book.

Integrating the Skills: Building Boardroom Competencies

Board leadership isn't about supervising from a distance anymore. It demands active engagement across strategy, risk, culture, and stakeholder dynamics—often simultaneously. Board members today must move fluently between advising, inquiring, and challenging leadership teams in environments where conditions evolve faster than oversight processes. Governance readiness depends not on isolated expertise but on the integration of leadership capabilities in real time.

Effective boardroom influence depends on combining skills under pressure. Key boardroom integrations include:

- *Strategic oversight meets adaptability:* Directors must maintain strategic clarity while helping organizations pivot when external realities shift.

- *Inquiry meets emotional intelligence*: Asking the right questions is important—but so is sensing how questions land within executive teams.

- *Technology awareness meets risk assessment*: Understanding digital trends is necessary, but integrating them into broader risk frameworks is where *board-level value is created.*

- *Decision-making discernment meets cultural fluency*: Supporting major organizational shifts requires balancing hard strategic logic with a deep understanding of cultural impacts.

Boardroom competencies aren't simply about subject matter expertise. They are about leadership integration—applying professional, personal, and technological capabilities simultaneously to strengthen organizational resilience. In today's landscape, credibility as a director depends not just on what you know but on how fluently you can navigate complexity when full control isn't part of the job description.

Evolving Case Study: David Chen's Realization

David Chen had served on boards for more than a decade. A former CFO with deep experience in corporate finance and strategic planning, he was known among his peers as a steady, thoughtful director—someone who could bring clarity to complex financial matters and offer sound perspective on organizational risk. At the board table, he was confident, respected, and rarely caught off guard. But during a recent strategy session for a mid-sized fintech company, that changed.

The discussion turned to artificial intelligence and its role in the company's evolving product roadmap. One director raised a question about how generative AI might reshape customer acquisition and underwriting. Another asked about emerging cybersecurity concerns tied to data architecture. The conversation quickly grew technical—touching on predictive analytics, model transparency, and AI governance frameworks.

David found himself unusually quiet. While he grasped the strategic implications, he realized he lacked the vocabulary—and fluency—to engage at the level the conversation now demanded. He had always considered himself informed, but this moment revealed that his understanding of emerging technologies hadn't kept pace with the board's growing oversight responsibilities.

That experience prompted a period of reflection. David began to question not just his digital literacy but whether there were other areas where his leadership approach had stalled. As he revisited his contributions across recent board engagements, he started to notice recurring blind spots—missed opportunities to lean into stakeholder engagement, hesitation in shaping long-term strategy, and a growing reliance on familiar strengths.

This moment would mark the beginning of a broader shift. Over the course of the chapters that follow, David's evolving case study will illustrate what it looks like for a seasoned director to reassess, reprioritize, and intentionally develop the modern skills required for effective governance in today's rapidly changing environment. His journey offers a lens through which any board member—regardless of experience—can explore their own path to leadership growth by developing not just individual skills, but the broader capabilities those skills unlock when applied in combination.

Chapter Summary

The evolution of leadership is not theoretical—it is imperative. In today's boardroom, success depends on a director's ability to integrate professional, personal, and technology skills into a dynamic and adaptive leadership profile. These 15 essential skills form the foundation from which boardroom competencies emerge—enabling directors to navigate disruption, provide strategic oversight, and engage with stakeholders in meaningful ways.

This chapter introduced the evolving case study of David Chen, a seasoned board member whose moment of realization—during a discussion on AI and cybersecurity—exposed a growing gap in his technology fluency. That moment became a catalyst for self-reflection and a deeper reassessment of how he applies his leadership skills across the boardroom context. As his journey unfolds, David's story will illustrate how leadership development must be ongoing, prioritized, and role specific.

In the next chapter, we'll explore how the role of the board member itself is evolving—expanding beyond financial oversight and compliance into a broader, more complex mandate. From technology governance to stakeholder leadership, today's directors face a growing set of expectations that demand a more modern approach to leadership—and a deeper understanding of where and how to apply the skills introduced in this chapter.

CHAPTER 2

THE EVOLVING ROLE OF TODAY'S BOARD MEMBER

The nature of board leadership is changing. Directors are no longer positioned simply as stewards of financial oversight or compliance. Today's boardrooms operate at the intersection of strategic disruption, digital transformation, stakeholder activism, and organizational culture—and board members are expected to lead across all of it, not just react to it.

In this environment, governance has evolved from supervision to strategic contribution. Directors must blend fiduciary responsibility with the ability to guide organizations through cycles of innovation, risk management, stakeholder shifts, and reputational complexity. Traditional experience still matters—but it is no longer sufficient on its own. Agility, fluency across disciplines, and a deeper leadership readiness are now required at the board level.

Board members are being asked to anticipate risks before formal frameworks exist, challenge leadership teams constructively without undermining operational confidence, and engage with technology and cultural dynamics in ways that strengthen—not destabilize—organizational resilience. The expectations around influence, inquiry, and strategic partnership have expanded dramatically, and effective directors must evolve alongside them.

This chapter builds from the leadership skills reintroduced earlier and frames how external forces are reshaping board effectiveness. We'll examine how directors can move beyond subject matter expertise toward integrated leadership competencies—skills activated intentionally, across moments where governance complexity doesn't wait for comfort zones to catch up. Because in today's boardrooms, leadership readiness isn't a credential—it's an active posture.

The Traditional Role of a Board Member: Foundations of Governance

Historically, the board's role was defined by structure, oversight, and specialization. Directors were recruited for their executive backgrounds—typically in finance, operations, or legal—and brought their expertise to committee-focused governance. The emphasis was on compliance, financial stewardship, and protecting shareholder value. In many cases, directors operated within clearly defined lanes, offering subject-matter input rather than broad-based leadership.

This model—while effective in more predictable eras—delivered meaningful value through focused execution. Boards ensured financial oversight, regulatory compliance, risk mitigation, CEO succession, and shareholder representation. These responsibilities provided structure and accountability, particularly in times of relative stability.

But as the business environment accelerated—and governance challenges became more interconnected, dynamic, and reputation-driven—the limitations of this approach became clear. Its compartmentalized structure often left boards unprepared for rapid disruption, unable to respond proactively to change, and ill-equipped to engage across complex stakeholder networks.

Take, for example, the board of Bolt Financial—a fintech startup that rocketed to an $11 billion valuation in just a few years. As the company chased growth, its leadership scaled aggressively: hiring hundreds of employees, expanding product scope, and pursuing a category-defining narrative. The board, composed largely of early investors and startup veterans, offered limited challenge to the founder's assumptions. Key areas—like unit economics, product-market fit, and go-to-market discipline—were either under scrutinized or deferred entirely to management.

When market conditions tightened in 2022, the gaps became impossible to ignore. Bolt was forced to lay off a third of its workforce and abandon core elements of its strategy. The board had not failed in its fiduciary duty per se—but it had failed in its leadership role. There was no meaningful integration of skills like visioning, technology awareness, translation, and communication—particularly in stakeholder contexts. What was missing wasn't knowledge or tenure—it was a cohesive leadership competency: the ability to synthesize across domains and lead through complexity with clarity and credibility.

That's the shift more boards are now confronting: the realization that modern governance demands not just oversight—but the active development and integration of contemporary leadership skills.

Expanding the Mandate: The Contemporary Board Member

The role of the board has undergone a fundamental transformation. Today's directors are no longer defined solely by what they oversee but by how they lead. The modern board is expected to operate as a strategic thought partner—one that brings foresight, fluency, and agility to a governance landscape marked by disruption and complexity.

This expanded mandate reflects a shift from traditional, committee-bound oversight to enterprise-level leadership. Boards are now responsible for ensuring that organizations are not only financially sound but also strategically future-proofed, technologically resilient, ethically grounded, and socially accountable. This evolution demands more than specialized knowledge—it requires integrated leadership capabilities that align with the demands of modern governance.

As boards face these expanded expectations, it becomes clear that traditional roles and skills alone are insufficient. The landscape of governance has shifted, and seven forces stand out as particularly significant in driving the evolution of board responsibilities. These seven forces represent what are arguably the most critical challenges shaping what boards must now do—and how directors must adapt to meet those demands effectively.

Key Factors in Determining Which Skills to Prioritize

1. The Rise of Stakeholder Capitalism

Modern boards must engage a broader set of stakeholders—including employees, customers, regulators, and communities—not just shareholders. Long-term value is now inseparable from reputation, trust, and purpose.

To navigate this expanded lens, board members must cultivate strong stakeholder alignment as a competency, supported by the following skills. These skills are foundational for modern governance, but how they are emphasized and applied will depend on the specific demands of the organization and its current challenges.

- *Curiosity (personal)* — actively seeking diverse viewpoints to inform decision making
- *Emotional Intelligence (personal)* — understanding stakeholder needs and tensions with empathy

- *Communication (professional)* — clearly articulating direction and values across stakeholder groups
- *Decision Making (professional)* — balancing trade-offs between short-term gains and long-term outcomes
- *Technology Awareness (technology)* — understanding how digital transparency and media shape public perception

Familiar Example: Airbnb's Stakeholder-Centric Strategy

Airbnb's board helped navigate a wave of post-pandemic stakeholder scrutiny—balancing host community needs, housing policy pressure, and brand trust. Their efforts to embed stakeholder impact into strategic planning showcased the board's role in ensuring purpose and profit remain aligned. Beyond setting policy, directors worked with leadership to anticipate regulatory shifts, rebuild community engagement trust, and ensure stakeholder concerns directly influenced the company's long-term risk strategy—solidifying governance credibility during a period of accelerated pressure.

2. Technology and Digital Disruption

Boards must now provide oversight on digital transformation, innovation strategy, cybersecurity, and AI governance—areas that touch every function, not just IT.

To do so effectively, board members need to develop digital foresight as a competency, drawing on the following skills. While these skills are critical for navigating the digital landscape, how they are applied will depend on the organization's technological maturity, its level of digital transformation, and the role of the director in this process.

- *Technology Awareness (technology)* — staying current on emerging technologies and their implications
- *Technology Objectivity (technology)* — evaluating tools and trends through a strategic, unbiased lens
- *Visioning (professional)* — connecting technology decisions to long-term business value

23

- *Adaptability (personal)* — evolving with emerging digital landscapes and operating models

Familiar Example: Nvidia's Strategic Tech Foresight

Nvidia's board has played a pivotal role in the company's rise as a leader in AI infrastructure—guiding strategic bets on generative AI, data centers, and developer ecosystems. Their fluency in tech trends and ability to connect them to long-term value demonstrates modern digital governance in action. Beyond investment foresight, directors worked with executive leadership to challenge assumptions about platform scalability, anticipate ethical AI governance pressures, and integrate cybersecurity resilience into long-term strategic planning—ensuring Nvidia's growth remained credible in a rapidly shifting digital environment.

3. Crisis Preparedness and Response

Crisis is now a governance constant—from cyberattacks to geopolitical tensions to reputational backlash. Boards must lead through volatility, not just react to it.

Crisis leadership requires the following skills, which empower board members to make informed decisions in moments of high pressure. While all directors must develop these skills, the application will depend on the type of crisis, the organization's resilience, and the director's unique role in crisis management.

- *Problem Solving (professional)* — identifying core issues and evaluating resolution pathways
- *Decision Making (professional)* — acting decisively under pressure, guided by values and context
- *Resilience (personal)* — maintaining focus and composure in high-stakes situations
- *Authenticity (personal)* — showing consistency, transparency, and trustworthiness during disruption

- *Technology Application (technology)* — leveraging tools to manage and communicate through crises

Familiar Example: Okta's Crisis Response and Recovery

Following a major cybersecurity breach, Okta's board quickly mobilized to guide crisis communications, engage regulators, and rebuild trust with enterprise clients—reinforcing the need for directors to pair technical acumen with human-centered leadership in moments of high scrutiny. Beyond immediate response, the board worked to embed lessons learned into governance practices—updating cybersecurity oversight protocols, recalibrating disclosure strategies, and strengthening board-management crisis simulation exercises to ensure greater resilience for future incidents.

4. Regulatory Complexity and Governance Transparency

From ESG disclosure mandates to AI ethics and antitrust concerns, boards face a more intense regulatory environment—and rising demands for clarity and transparency from investors, media, and policymakers.

Navigating these complexities requires a high level of governance integrity, underpinned by the following skills. These are essential for ensuring clarity and alignment with regulatory expectations, but the degree to which each skill is applied will depend on the organization's regulatory environment and the director's role in overseeing compliance.

- *Translation (professional)* — converting complex regulatory shifts into actionable oversight

- *Communication (professional)* — ensuring clear dialogue with stakeholders and regulators

- *Coaching (personal)* — supporting executive teams in navigating evolving expectations

- *Authenticity (personal)* — modeling ethical clarity and alignment between board values and behavior

- *Technology Awareness (technology)* — overseeing systems that support compliance, reporting, and risk mitigation

Familiar Example: Meta's Governance Under Pressure

Meta's board has faced growing pressure around platform regulation, AI safety, and data governance. By restructuring oversight committees and elevating governance transparency in response to stakeholder and regulatory demands, the board demonstrated the evolving role directors play in balancing innovation with accountability. In parallel, directors worked to strengthen board-level risk governance frameworks—ensuring that emerging regulatory requirements on data privacy, platform fairness, and algorithmic accountability were proactively anticipated rather than reactively managed, reinforcing board leadership credibility amid evolving global scrutiny.

5. Geopolitical Risk and Supply Chain Volatility

Global instability, trade disruption, and resource scarcity have moved supply chain resilience and geopolitical awareness into core boardroom conversations.

Strategic risk oversight in this context depends on the following skills, which are essential for anticipating and mitigating future disruptions. The application of these skills will vary based on the director's role in global strategy and the level of complexity in the organization's operations.

- *Visioning (professional)* — anticipating future disruptions and scenario planning for resilience
- *Problem Solving (professional)* — addressing systemic weaknesses with agility
- *Adaptability (personal)* — shifting oversight priorities as the global landscape evolves
- *Curiosity (personal)* — engaging with global and cross-industry signals

- *Technology Application (technology)* — leveraging analytics and AI for visibility and forecasting

Familiar Example: TSMC's Governance-Driven Supply Chain Strategy

Taiwan Semiconductor Manufacturing Company (TSMC)'s board has played a pivotal role in reshaping the company's supply chain strategy in response to rising geopolitical tensions between China and Taiwan. Their leadership helped drive major diversification efforts—investing in semiconductor fabrication facilities in the U.S., Japan, and Europe—to reduce concentration risks. The board's proactive governance approach highlighted not only risk mitigation but also strategic foresight: aligning operational expansion with global national security concerns and protecting long-term organizational resilience. TSMC's example illustrates how modern boards must anticipate geopolitical volatility early rather than react to crises after supply chains are compromised.

6. Workforce Transformation and Culture Oversight

As work models evolve, boards must now ensure their organizations can attract, retain, and empower a modern, purpose-driven workforce. Culture oversight is no longer optional—it's a core governance responsibility.

Directors must develop the following competencies in workforce engagement. The need for these skills will depend on the organizational culture, leadership structure, and the board's specific role in shaping the workforce strategy.

- *Coaching (personal)*— fostering executive development and cultural clarity
- *Emotional Intelligence (personal)* — attuning to team dynamics, engagement, and morale
- *Motivation (professional)* — aligning culture with purpose and performance

- *Technology Awareness (technology)* — understanding how digital tools shape workplace experience
- *Authenticity (personal)* — setting the tone for inclusive, values-aligned leadership

Familiar Example: Shopify's Culture-Focused Governance

Shopify's board helped steward a culture evolution during its shift to a fully remote operating model—emphasizing executive resilience, team connection, and reimagined performance standards. The board's involvement reflected the increasing need for directors to lead with empathy and adaptability in talent strategy. Beyond policy shifts, directors worked to ensure that digital employee experience, mental health support, and long-term cultural cohesion became core governance priorities—recognizing that sustainable workforce resilience now demands ongoing leadership engagement, not episodic interventions.

7. Investor Pressure and Long-term Value Stewardship

Activist investors, institutional shareholders, and proxy advisors are exerting more pressure than ever on boards to clarify strategic direction, demonstrate accountability, and deliver sustainable performance. This scrutiny is broader than financials—it includes culture, ESG, governance structure, and leadership continuity.

To address this growing pressure, boards must develop a strategic influence mindset built on the following skills. The application of these skills will vary depending on the nature of the investor pressure, the board's role in shareholder communication, and the long-term strategy of the organization.

- *Decision Making (professional)* — weighing investor input against long-term organizational strategy
- *Communication (professional)* — engaging constructively with investors, analysts, and governance advisors
- *Visioning (professional)* — maintaining clarity on long-term direction and how board decisions support it

- *Authenticity (personal)* — building trust through consistency and transparency
- *Technology Objectivity (technology)* — evaluating performance metrics, analytics, and shareholder data without bias

Familiar Example: Disney's Activist Response and Strategic Poise

In recent years, Disney's board faced sustained activist pressure from Nelson Peltz and other investors pushing for governance changes and succession clarity. Rather than react defensively, the board proactively addressed strategic concerns, publicly reaffirmed long-term plans, and made structural moves that reflected both investor feedback and board conviction—demonstrating the importance of calm, confident influence under scrutiny. Beyond tactical responses, directors remained disciplined in stakeholder communications, signaling board unity, reinforcing leadership credibility, and protecting long-term strategic priorities without surrendering core governance principles to short-term activist demands.

As these forces reshape governance expectations, directors must move beyond historical expertise and legacy oversight. The modern board member must be a leadership integrator—capable of synthesizing core skills into dynamic, role-specific competencies that guide governance forward.

This is not a theoretical shift—it is a practical one. Boards that fail to evolve risk falling behind stakeholder expectations, regulatory pressures, and strategic opportunities. Boards that succeed will build lasting value by translating complexity into clarity and disruption into direction.

The Leadership Equation Reframed

The seven forces outlined in this chapter aren't simply trends for boards to monitor—they are structural shifts that demand a new leadership equation. Each force challenges long-held assumptions about how directors add value. Each one calls for a more integrated, forward-facing boardroom presence.

What these forces truly require are updated competencies: the ability to guide organizations through complexity, ambiguity, and disruption with clarity and credibility. But competencies don't appear on a résumé—they are built. And they are built through the deliberate application of modern leadership skills.

The path from leadership pressure to boardroom performance is clear: External forces create new challenges. Competencies reflect the ability to meet them. And competencies are built by developing and integrating the right leadership skills.

In the chapters ahead, we'll explore how directors can engage with this model more intentionally—starting with how to identify which skills matter most in their board role and how to focus their development where it will have the greatest impact.

But first, we return to David Chen, whose own leadership equation is about to be challenged—and recalibrated.

Evolving Case Study: David Chen's Competency Gap

The discomfort David felt in that AI discussion didn't fade—it deepened. What began as unease quickly became reflection. He started looking more closely at other moments where he had felt on the margins: a tense exchange around labor practices, a missed opportunity to shape the company's talent strategy, an ESG discussion that veered into social impact.

In each case, he recognized the same pattern—not just a gap in knowledge, but a shortfall in essential skills. Technology awareness was part of it. So were adaptability, emotional intelligence, and communication.

Behind those gaps was something even more important: a missing leadership competency.

That realization came into sharper focus during a private follow-up session with a lead investor. The investor questioned whether the board, as currently composed, had the leadership range required to govern innovation, ethics, and organizational risk in a tech-driven world. David knew the question wasn't aimed directly at him—but it landed that way.

For the first time, he felt genuinely uncertain about his ability to lead at the level modern governance now demanded.

It wasn't a crisis. But it was a reckoning—a moment that demanded not just reflection but action.

In the weeks that followed, he continued to reflect—not just on where he was falling short, but on why. He began to see that the forces reshaping the boardroom—ranging from digital disruption to stakeholder capitalism—weren't just shifting what boards talked about. They were redefining what effective board leadership demanded.

His challenge wasn't a lack of experience—it was the absence of a boardroom competency: the ability to navigate decisions that spanned technology, people, and purpose with confidence and clarity. And that kind of competency wouldn't emerge automatically.

It would have to be rebuilt—with intention.

Chapter Summary

The role of the board has evolved well beyond financial oversight and regulatory compliance. Today's directors are expected to lead with strategic insight, cultural fluency, and technological awareness in response to mounting external pressures—ranging from stakeholder activism and digital disruption to regulatory complexity and workforce transformation. These forces are not just influencing governance—they are redefining it.

To meet this moment, board members must develop competencies: integrated capabilities formed through the deliberate application of multiple modern leadership skills. While all 15 essential skills introduced in Chapter 1 remain relevant, impact comes not from mastering them all equally, but from combining the right skills in the right context to address the forces at play. Competencies—not credentials—are now the true measure of boardroom readiness.

David Chen's experience illustrates this shift. His growing awareness of multiple skill gaps—from technology awareness to stakeholder engagement—signals a broader realization: Experience alone is no longer enough. The chapters ahead will explore how directors can assess their own leadership profile, prioritize the skills that matter most, and begin building the competencies required for modern board effectiveness.

CHAPTER 3

IDENTIFYING AND PRIORITIZING THE ESSENTIAL BOARDROOM LEADERSHIP SKILLS

With governance responsibilities expanding and disruption accelerating, today's board members face more complexity than ever before. In Chapter 1, we introduced the 15 modern leadership skills that form the foundation of boardroom effectiveness. Chapter 2 illustrated how those skills—when thoughtfully combined—enable directors to form the competencies needed to address key governance forces, from digital transformation to stakeholder activism to investor scrutiny.

But acknowledging the need for leadership evolution is only the beginning. Board members must also determine which skills to prioritize based on their specific board context, individual role, and personal growth edge. Not every director needs to master every skill equally. What matters most is intentional alignment: identifying the skill combinations that build the competencies most relevant to the board's current challenges and long-term direction. This is especially important given the seven forces introduced in Chapter 2—each of which requires boards to respond with targeted, role-specific leadership competencies.

In this chapter, we explore how directors can navigate that prioritization process. We'll introduce a practical framework to help board members assess their role, evaluate the forces shaping their board's agenda, and choose the skills that will yield the greatest governance impact. Through this lens, leadership development becomes not just a personal imperative but a strategic, board-level contribution.

Key Factors in Determining Which Skills to Prioritize

Prioritizing skill development as a board member requires more than self-reflection or intuition. It demands a strategic lens—one that considers the evolving role you play on the board, the challenges facing the organization, and where your leadership can create the most leverage. It also requires awareness of the broader governance landscape—the structural forces reshaping board expectations—and the competencies needed to meet them.

The following five factors offer a practical framework for identifying which of the 15 essential leadership skills deserve focused attention—and for aligning your development priorities with the realities shaping your board's agenda.

1. Board Role and Committee Responsibilities

The skills most relevant to you may depend on the seat you hold. A director serving on the audit committee may need to deepen their translation and decision-making capabilities. A governance committee chair might benefit more from coaching and adaptability. Prioritization starts with understanding how your current responsibilities shape the kind of leadership you're expected to bring.

But effective board leadership goes beyond technical committee expertise. It's about recognizing how committee assignments create strategic influence pathways—or expose gaps.

Audit oversight impacts credibility with investors. Governance leadership shapes succession planning and stakeholder trust. Compensation committee dynamics affect culture and long-term organizational health. Your leadership priorities should reflect not just what your committee manages but how your influence can stabilize or stretch the organization.

Not all committee roles carry the same leadership demands at all times. Strategic risk may be dormant one year and critical the next. Culture oversight may surge to the forefront following M&A activity or a leadership transition. Staying attuned to how governance priorities shift—and how your own leadership profile must evolve in parallel—is essential to maintaining boardroom credibility and effectiveness.

- *Ask yourself:* Where am I expected to contribute most right now? Which of the 15 skills align most closely with my committee or board leadership responsibilities?
- *Practical example:* A director newly appointed to lead the compensation committee prioritizes authenticity and emotional intelligence to better support CEO evaluation and culture oversight.

2. Organizational Context

What your organization is navigating today should shape which skills you prioritize. A company undergoing a digital transformation may require directors to lean into technology awareness and visioning, while a business facing reputational risk might call for communication and resilience. The most relevant skills are those that help you support the board's oversight of the business in its current—and future—state.

But organizational context isn't static. Strategic challenges evolve—and board leadership priorities must evolve with them. A board that once focused heavily on growth oversight might find itself needing to prioritize risk management after a market downturn.

A company that once centered around operational scale may now require cultural transformation to retain top talent. Directors must be able to read organizational shifts early and realign their leadership profile accordingly.

Effective board leadership means anticipating what the business will need—not just responding once the need becomes urgent. Directors who stay locked in a fixed leadership posture risk becoming disconnected from the organization's emerging priorities. Prioritizing skills dynamically, in response to organizational signals, is one of the clearest marks of boardroom agility—and one of the clearest differentiators of boardroom credibility.

- *Ask yourself:* What is the most pressing issue facing our board today—and which skills are most essential to help the board lead through this issue?

- *Practical example:* A healthcare company preparing for M&A (mergers and acquisitions) activity prompts a director to focus on visioning and communication to help guide strategic integration conversations.

3. Peer Strengths and Gaps

Boards operate as teams. If your board already has multiple directors fluent in financial oversight but lacks strength in areas like technology objectivity or stakeholder communication, that may influence where you can add unique value. Prioritization should take into account complementarity, not just personal interest.

Effective governance depends on the collective leadership profile of the board—not just the capabilities of individual directors. Understanding where the board is strong, where it is over-indexed, and where critical gaps exist is essential to strategic board effectiveness. A director's leadership contribution is magnified when it fills a gap that would otherwise expose the organization to risk, stakeholder friction, or blind spots in strategic oversight.

Stepping into leadership spaces where the board is thin isn't just a personal growth opportunity—it's a governance imperative. Directors who are willing to expand their leadership skill set in response to evolving board needs strengthen both the organization's resilience and the board's credibility. Prioritization becomes not just a question of where you want to lead, but where the organization most needs you to lead.

- *Ask yourself:* Where does my skill set complement—or duplicate—the capabilities of my peers? Where could I step up to fill a board-level gap?

- *Practical example:* A director with baseline tech knowledge leans into building stronger technology objectivity after realizing the board is over-indexed on operations experience.

4. Personal Growth Edge

Some skills may stretch you—and that's the point. You might have underdeveloped areas that are critical in today's governance environment. A director who has avoided culture conversations may benefit from building emotional intelligence or authenticity. Someone less confident in public settings may need to strengthen communication or resilience. Prioritizing growth in these areas can elevate your boardroom presence and unlock new contributions.

Leadership growth at the board level isn't about chasing perfection. It's about recognizing where incremental improvement can unlock disproportionate influence and trust. Sometimes the areas that feel least natural—managing cultural oversight, leading digital governance conversations, engaging in difficult stakeholder dynamics—are exactly the spaces where leadership evolution creates the most boardroom impact.

Directors who stretch into discomfort expand their ability to stabilize boards during volatility, build credibility across diverse stakeholders, and guide executive teams through uncertainty. Prioritizing leadership growth isn't just about personal development—it's about board readiness. Modern governance requires directors who are willing to evolve as the complexity of the environment demands.

- *Ask yourself:* Which skill feels a little uncomfortable—but important? Where do I sense the most opportunity for personal leadership growth?

- *Practical example:* A seasoned CFO begins developing coaching and stakeholder communication skills after recognizing how much her voice shapes the tone of executive dialogue.

5. Long-term Governance Trends

Some skills may not feel urgent, but they will soon become essential. Directors who invest in emotional intelligence, technology awareness, and authenticity today will be better positioned for the evolving demands of ESG scrutiny, AI governance, and inclusive stakeholder leadership. Strategic prioritization also requires foresight.

Governance complexity isn't standing still. Pressures around sustainability reporting, algorithmic ethics, workforce transparency, and stakeholder capitalism are moving from future trends to immediate boardroom realities. Directors who wait until these shifts are fully mainstreamed will find themselves reacting from a position of weakness rather than leading with informed intent. Anticipating the leadership capabilities future governance will require is part of today's strategic responsibility.

Board effectiveness over the next decade will not be determined solely by financial oversight or compliance strength. It will be shaped by a director's ability to lead through ambiguity, build trust across evolving stakeholder networks, and navigate complexity without full precedents or playbooks. Investing in forward-looking leadership skills today creates a governance posture ready for the complexity of tomorrow.

- *Ask yourself*: Which skills might not be critical yet but will be essential in the next two to three years? What will governance look like as the board's role continues to evolve?
- *Practical example*: A first-time director invests in adaptability and technology awareness after recognizing how AI and geopolitical risk are reshaping the company's industry.

Prioritizing the right skills is a critical step—but even with the best framework, it's easy for directors to fall into familiar traps. Sometimes the misstep is subtle: defaulting to what's familiar, overlooking areas of discomfort, or mistaking activity for progress. The goal isn't perfection—it's intentionality. The next section explores some of the most common pitfalls board members encounter during skill prioritization—and how to avoid them.

Avoiding Common Pitfalls in Skill Development

Even with a clear framework in place, board members can fall into familiar traps when deciding which skills to prioritize. In a fast-moving governance environment, it's easy to mistake activity for progress—or to default to what feels comfortable. The following are five common missteps directors make during the prioritization process—and how to avoid them in the pursuit of boardroom competencies that matter.

1. Choosing What's Comfortable Over What's Strategic

Many directors focus on deepening strengths they already have rather than building new capabilities that respond to current board needs. Comfort can become a trap: Doubling down on financial expertise, operational review, or audit mastery may feel productive—

39

but it can leave critical leadership voids unaddressed. Governance today demands a broader range of leadership fluency. Directors who resist stretching into less familiar skill areas—such as stakeholder engagement, technology fluency, or culture oversight—risk limiting their boardroom influence and missing opportunities to stabilize organizations during volatility.

- *Practical example:* A finance-focused director prioritized deeper audit knowledge, even as the board struggled with stakeholder trust and reputational risk—leaving a leadership void in public engagement.

- *Proactive tip:* That director might have benefited from stretching into less familiar skill areas—like communication or authenticity—where leadership was urgently needed but underrepresented on the board.

2. Focusing Too Broadly Without Clear Priorities

Trying to "cover everything" leads to shallow progress. Without clarity, directors may dabble across multiple skills without building meaningful competency in any. Broad ambition without focus often creates the illusion of development—but without the depth or durability boards require. Leadership growth at the board level isn't about touching every skill—it's about intentionally deepening the capabilities that stabilize governance under complexity. When everything is a priority, nothing actually moves—and critical leadership gaps remain exposed just when board resilience is most needed.

- *Practical example:* One director set a goal to improve in eight skill areas over the course of a year—but never progressed meaningfully on any of them, leaving development fragmented and unfocused.

- *Proactive tip:* A more effective approach for that director might have been to choose one or two high-leverage skills and go deeper—ensuring tangible progress and reinforcing learning through real-time board application.

3. Confusing Familiarity with Mastery

It's common to assume fluency in a skill because you've used it in another context. But board leadership often requires applying skills differently than in executive roles. Familiarity with communication, decision making, or stakeholder management doesn't automatically translate when the leadership environment shifts from operational control to governance influence. Directors must recognize that even well-developed capabilities need recalibration to fit the unique dynamics, constraints, and expectations of board leadership. Mistaking familiarity for true boardroom mastery risks weakening influence at precisely the moments when leadership clarity is most critical.

- *Practical example:* A former COO assumed stakeholder communication was a strength—until a misjudged message during a governance change revealed critical blind spots.

- *Proactive tip:* That director could have benefited from feedback or peer coaching to pressure-test how their communication approach translated into the boardroom—rather than assuming past success equaled current readiness.

4. Ignoring the Interplay Between Skills

Directors sometimes treat the 15 essential skills as standalone elements rather than recognizing how they combine to form high-impact competencies. Boardroom leadership rarely tests one skill in isolation. Strategic influence often emerges from the integration of capabilities—pairing technical fluency with emotional intelligence or combining decisiveness with authentic communication. Directors who over-index on a single skill risk creating blind spots, missing relational dynamics, or weakening board cohesion. Modern governance demands the ability to move fluidly across domains, blending skills to create credible, situational leadership when full control isn't an option.

- *Practical example:* A tech-savvy board member leaned heavily on technology awareness but lacked the emotional intelligence to connect that expertise to people and culture priorities.

- *Proactive tip:* For that board member, pairing technical insight with relational leadership—such as emotional intelligence or coaching—might have increased their overall influence and impact in the room.

5. Waiting for a Crisis to Guide Development

Some directors delay intentional growth until it's urgently needed; by then, the opportunity for proactive leadership has already passed. Reactivity undermines board credibility and weakens governance influence at the moments when it matters most. Building new leadership capabilities under crisis conditions is harder, riskier, and more visible. Effective directors anticipate pressure points before they escalate—forecasting likely areas of scrutiny, stakeholder friction, or leadership challenge, and building strength early. Skill development isn't just about improving personal effectiveness; it's about strengthening organizational resilience before leadership gaps become vulnerabilities.

- *Practical example:* A board ignored early signs of regulatory scrutiny and only invested in governance fluency after a high-stakes compliance issue went public.

- *Proactive tip:* That board might have avoided reactive decision making by forecasting likely areas of oversight demand—and developing those skills in advance of visible risk.

Leading effectively at the board level isn't just about knowing what to prioritize—it's about staying alert to where leadership gaps can quietly widen. As the pressures on governance grow more complex, the ability to step beyond familiar strengths becomes essential. Directors who move intentionally toward new leadership challenges strengthen not only their own credibility but the resilience of the board as a whole. David Chen was beginning to recognize that. His experience wasn't obsolete—but it wasn't sufficient on its own. The forces reshaping board leadership demanded something more—and it was time for David to decide where he would start.

Evolving Case Study: David Chen Begins to Prioritize

David Chen didn't need more confirmation that something had shifted. After the investor meeting that left him rethinking his boardroom relevance, he began to reflect with greater focus. He had already identified that his gap wasn't about a single issue—it was about building a new kind of leadership competency, one better suited to the forces now shaping the board's agenda. But knowing that wasn't the same as knowing where to start.

He turned to the five-factor framework introduced earlier in this chapter—not as a checklist, but as a lens to assess himself with intention.

1. *Board Role and Committee Responsibilities:* As chair of the audit and risk committee, David's responsibilities were expanding beyond financial oversight. Decision making and translation still mattered, but so did his ability to contribute to broader conversations around strategy, culture, and innovation.

2. *Organizational Context:* The company was in the middle of a high-stakes digital pivot. AI investments were rising, talent was harder to retain, and regulators were asking more questions. The board's ability to lead through transformation was now a strategic asset—and a visible one.

3. *Peer Strengths and Gaps:* His fellow directors had deep legal and operational experience, but few demonstrated confidence when it came to emerging technologies or stakeholder engagement. The gaps were real, and he saw where his voice could matter more—if he developed the right skills.

4. *Personal Growth Edge:* David had long relied on financial fluency to navigate complexity. But when conversations turned to culture or long-term stakeholder trust, he often withdrew. He began to see that this pattern wasn't just a style choice—it was limiting his leadership.

5. *Long-term Governance Trends:* The more he engaged with emerging issues, the more he understood that directors would be expected to speak credibly about AI, connect across stakeholder divides, and help shape rather than react to disruption. That wasn't the future—it was already here.

By the end of this process, David had identified three priorities that spanned all three leadership domains:

- *Technology awareness,* to engage meaningfully in AI and data oversight
- *Communication,* with a focus on high-expectation stakeholder audiences
- *Authenticity,* to show up more consistently and credibly in complex, values-driven discussions

These weren't isolated skills. Together, they formed the foundation of a new boardroom competency—one rooted not in familiarity, but in relevance. David didn't yet know how he would develop each of them. But he had moved from uncertainty to clarity. And for the first time in months, he felt like he had direction.

Chapter Summary

In today's governance environment, board members must do more than possess broad leadership skills—they must actively prioritize the ones that matter most. This chapter introduced a practical framework to help directors determine which of the 15 essential leadership skills will have the greatest impact based on their board role, organizational challenges, peer dynamics, and long-term governance trends. Prioritization isn't about addressing every gap—it's about identifying the skill combinations that build the competencies most needed to meet today's most pressing governance demands.

Through practical examples and a series of common development pitfalls, we explored how directors often default to what feels familiar rather than what's most strategic. Many spread their development too thin, overestimate mastery in familiar areas, or fail to recognize how individual skills combine to form boardroom competencies. Avoiding these traps is essential for directors who want to lead with clarity, depth, and adaptability in a rapidly changing environment.

David Chen's case study brought this challenge to life. As a seasoned board member facing new expectations, David realized that his traditional expertise no longer covered the full scope of modern governance. By applying the prioritization framework, he identified technology awareness, communication, and authenticity—focusing his communication skill on stakeholder-facing challenges. In the next chapter, we'll explore how board members like David can move from clarity to action—building the competencies they've prioritized through intentional, role-aligned development.

CHAPTER 4

FROM AWARENESS TO ACTION—DEVELOPING
ESSENTIAL BOARDROOM LEADERSHIP SKILLS

Having identified and prioritized the leadership skills that matter most, the next challenge for board members is bridging the gap between awareness and action. Knowing which skills to focus on is only part of the equation—directors must also commit to intentional, structured development. Without it, even the most experienced board members risk stagnation, relying on outdated expertise rather than building the skills required to stay relevant and lead effectively in a rapidly evolving business environment.

Unlike executives, who develop leadership skills through daily operational decisions, board members must take a different approach. Their role is centered on influence rather than execution, requiring them to cultivate expertise in anticipation of key governance moments—not just in response to them. This means directors must be proactive in their own development, continually refining the skills that will position them to contribute meaningfully—when it counts most.

In this chapter, we explore a contemporary approach to board-level leadership development. From self-directed learning and peer-driven mentorship to formal governance programs and expert coaching, we outline a practical framework for building the essential skills introduced in Chapter 1. These strategies are designed to help directors deepen their capabilities across the professional, personal, and technology domains—laying the groundwork for the competencies needed to navigate today's evolving governance demands.

The Need for a Contemporary Approach to Board Leadership Development

Traditional board training has often emphasized financial oversight, regulatory compliance, and governance processes. While these foundations remain important, they are no longer sufficient on their own. Today's directors must expand their leadership toolkit to include modern skills like technology awareness, adaptability, visioning, and communication—especially in high-stakes stakeholder contexts. Without a shift in how board members learn and grow, many will struggle to keep pace with the demands of modern governance.

The contemporary board member must embrace a continuous, multidimensional learning model—one that reflects the speed, scope, and complexity of the challenges they face. That means leveraging a range of development resources: AI-enabled learning platforms, real-time simulations, digital content, peer mentoring, and specialized coaching—all aligned to the professional, personal, and technology domains outlined in Chapter 1.

To remain effective, directors must adopt a diversified development strategy—balancing independent learning with collaborative exploration and formalized education. The four pathways outlined in the sections that follow provide a practical, flexible framework for building the right skills with depth and focus. When pursued intentionally, these approaches help directors grow in ways that are both personal and practical—and in doing so, lay the foundation for more integrated, high-impact boardroom leadership.

Four Key Pathways for Board Member Leadership Development

There is no single blueprint for leadership development. Some directors prefer independent learning; others gain more from peer mentorship, structured programs, or one-on-one coaching. What matters is selecting the approaches that best support development of the specific skills that strengthen a director's ability to lead effectively in the boardroom.

Board leadership isn't built solely through knowledge acquisition—it's built through application under pressure. Modern governance demands fluency across disciplines, responsiveness to evolving stakeholder expectations, and the ability to integrate leadership skills in ways that stabilize organizations during complexity. Developing these capabilities intentionally, through the right mix of learning mechanisms, is now an essential part of sustaining board credibility.

The four pathways that follow offer a contemporary framework for skill building, each mapped to the three core domains—professional, personal, and technology—introduced in Chapter 1. When used in combination, these strategies help directors build not only individual skills but also the integrated competencies required to meet today's evolving governance demands.

1. Self-directed Learning—Building Personal Accountability

Many board members begin with self-directed learning—an independent, proactive approach that allows directors to stay ahead of emerging trends and governance challenges. In an era where complexity is increasing exponentially, self-directed learning is no longer optional—it is foundational. Directors who fail to take charge of their own development risk falling behind, particularly in areas like AI governance, cybersecurity, and stakeholder engagement.

Board leadership demands fluency across domains that don't always align neatly with past professional experience. Directors must build strategic, relational, and digital capabilities intentionally—often without formal mandates or external prompts. Self-directed development allows board members to close emerging leadership gaps before they become governance vulnerabilities, reinforcing board effectiveness during periods of heightened complexity.

Self-directed learning is best for developing:

- *Professional skills* — visioning, decision making, problem solving
- *Technology skills* — technology awareness, technology application

By targeting these individual skills through curated content and independent study, directors can make tangible progress on their highest-priority development goals. This pathway reinforces personal accountability and allows for highly tailored skill building. While individual learning builds depth in specific domains, it also strengthens the director's ability to contribute in broader governance conversations—particularly those tied to digital disruption, regulatory complexity, and investor pressure.

Key Self-Directed Learning Methods

1. *AI-powered Learning Platforms* — digital tools that personalize board governance education. These platforms assess current knowledge and suggest tailored content, ensuring more targeted and efficient development

2. *Virtual Board Simulations* — scenario-based exercises that replicate high-stakes decision-making environments, such as regulatory investigations or activist investor

negotiations, helping directors refine strategic judgment under pressure

3. *Governance Podcasts and Webinars* — ongoing access to thought leadership and evolving perspectives on board-relevant topics, including ESG trends, digital ethics, and geopolitical risk

Familiar Example: Microsoft's Digital Upskilling for Directors

Microsoft's board has actively invested in self-directed technology development to support its oversight of AI and cloud transformation. Directors engaged in tailored learning on AI governance, cybersecurity, and digital ethics—reinforcing their technology awareness and application skills. This commitment to continuous self-development has positioned the board to better navigate forces like digital disruption, stakeholder expectations, and long-term value stewardship.

2. Peer Learning and Boardroom Exposure—Leveraging Experience

Boardroom effectiveness is shaped not just by what directors know but by how they learn from peers, challenge assumptions, and refine their leadership through shared experience. The most effective directors actively seek out opportunities to learn from other board members, cross-industry colleagues, and stakeholder groups. Peer-driven learning offers a dynamic and high-context approach to development—one that blends mentorship, committee work, and real-time exposure to emerging governance demands.

What distinguishes peer learning at the board level is its immediacy. Directors are exposed to strategic debates, risk assessments, stakeholder dilemmas, and governance recalibrations as they happen—not as case studies, but as live leadership experiences. The best learning often comes not from consensus, but from navigating disagreement, building trust, and sharpening judgment across different leadership styles and perspectives.

Peer learning is best for developing:

- *Personal skills* — coaching, emotional intelligence, authenticity

- *Professional skills* — communication and visioning, especially in stakeholder-facing scenarios

When approached with intention, peer learning becomes a powerful mechanism for developing the skills that allow directors to influence without control. It helps build real fluency across interpersonal, strategic, and stakeholder-facing domains—reinforcing a director's ability to lead through ambiguity, change, and challenge. These skill gains often intersect and accumulate, laying the groundwork for stronger contributions when navigating complex boardroom issues.

Key Peer Learning Strategies

1. *Reverse Mentoring* — Senior directors partner with younger, tech-native leaders to exchange insights on AI, sustainability, and evolving stakeholder expectations.

2. *Board Exchange Networks* — Cross-industry board participation helps directors import best practices and broaden governance perspective.

3. *Committee Participation* — Specialized roles on ESG, cybersecurity, or innovation committees offer practical exposure to boardroom priorities that demand fluency and flexibility.

4. *Board Retreats and Roundtables* — Modern retreats emphasize data-driven strategy, AI-enhanced scenario planning, and inclusive debate—often blending in-person and virtual dialogue across global geographies.

5. *Stakeholder Engagement* — Direct dialogue with regulators, institutional investors, and employees fosters

better decision making and transparency on issues that span financial and non-financial priorities.

Familiar Example: Adobe's Cross-generational Learning Model

Adobe's board has embraced reverse mentorship and stakeholder engagement as core leadership development tools. Seasoned directors are paired with next-generation leaders across product, design, and digital innovation to stay current on user-experience trends, ethical AI challenges, and inclusive governance. This peer-based learning model has helped Adobe's board sharpen its visioning and authenticity skills while better aligning strategy with stakeholder expectations in a fast-evolving tech landscape.

3. Structured Leadership Development—Formal Governance Education

While self-directed learning and peer exposure offer flexibility, some leadership skills require deeper structure and discipline. Formal governance education can provide board members with a comprehensive understanding of their evolving responsibilities—equipping them to navigate complex decision making, risk oversight, and digital transformation with greater confidence.

Unlike self-directed growth, structured learning imposes deliberate pacing and precision—offering directors the opportunity to challenge assumptions, refine judgment, and integrate new leadership habits systematically. The discipline of a formal learning environment forces engagement beyond comfort zones and broadens a director's capacity to respond credibly under public, regulatory, and stakeholder scrutiny.

Structured education is best for developing:

- *Professional skills* — visioning, translation, decision making
- *Technology skills* — technology objectivity, technology application

Structured development helps directors deepen essential skills through immersive learning—not just expanding knowledge but building real fluency in how those skills are applied in high-stakes governance scenarios. It is particularly effective when addressing forces like regulatory complexity, crisis preparedness, and digital disruption—where confidence, clarity, and composure matter most. When paired with real-time board responsibilities, this form of development allows directors to connect formal learning directly to the issues their boards are navigating.

Key Governance Education Programs

1. *AI and Digital Governance Certifications* — executive courses that prepare directors to oversee digital transformation, data ethics, and cybersecurity risk without defaulting to management's expertise

2. *Crisis Leadership and Scenario Planning Workshops* — immersive training that strengthens board-level decision making during events such as cyberattacks, activist campaigns, or regulatory fallout

3. *Board Simulations* — interactive, real-time decision-making exercises that replicate governance dilemmas, such as balancing shareholder demands with long-term strategy or responding to ESG scrutiny.

4. *Global Board Training Programs* — international sessions that offer cross-border perspectives on sustainability reporting, geopolitical risk, and inclusive governance practices.

Familiar Example: Mastercard's Structured Director Education

Mastercard's board has invested heavily in formal director education, including cross-functional workshops on cybersecurity oversight, scenario planning, and data governance. These structured sessions not only enhanced the board's technology objectivity and decision-making skills—they also helped align directors around long-term strategic priorities in a rapidly shifting regulatory environment. This approach has helped directors strengthen their individual skills while reinforcing the board's collective ability to lead with focus and foresight.

4. Expert Coaching and Third-party Development—Personalized Growth

For some board members, the most effective way to accelerate skill development is through personalized coaching. Executive coaches, governance advisors, and third-party specialists provide targeted, one-on-one support to help directors sharpen the leadership skills most critical to their boardroom effectiveness.

Personalized development allows directors to work through specific leadership challenges in a confidential environment— addressing communication gaps, sharpening decision frameworks, or deepening adaptability without the scrutiny of full board dynamics. It transforms leadership growth from a broad aspiration into precise, context-driven action, tailored to both the organization's needs and the director's evolving role.

Expert coaching is best for developing:

- Personal skills — adaptability, resilience, emotional intelligence
- Technology skills — technology application, technology awareness

Expert coaching helps directors move from general awareness to precise skill development—supporting focused growth in areas where clarity, feedback, and personal context matter most. This pathway is particularly valuable when addressing governance forces such as investor scrutiny, stakeholder capitalism, and crisis response— moments that demand sharp communication, adaptability, and sound judgment. By building targeted skills through a personalized lens, directors can strengthen their contribution in the most high-leverage areas of board service.

Key Coaching and Expert-led Development Options

1. *One-on-One Coaching* — personalized guidance to enhance high-stakes communication, adaptability, and decision making under pressure.

2. *Digital Fluency Training with AI Advisors* — tailored instruction that helps directors ask better questions, evaluate AI proposals, and understand the implications of emerging technologies.

3. *Board Effectiveness Assessments* — objective third-party evaluations that identify development areas and support better alignment between board performance and strategy.

4. *Customized Director Development Plans* — roadmaps that link an individual's leadership growth directly to organizational priorities and board composition.

Familiar Example: Intuit's Personalized Development Strategy

Intuit has leveraged targeted coaching and third-party development to strengthen its board's oversight of innovation and risk. Directors participated in customized sessions on AI governance, data privacy, and strategic communication—focusing on how to engage confidently in fast-evolving tech and stakeholder landscapes. This personalized approach helped directors build the specific skills they needed—such as adaptability and technology application—while enhancing their influence in boardroom conversations that matter most.

The Final Step: Building a Custom Development Roadmap

Boardroom leadership isn't defined by tenure—it's shaped by intentional growth. In an era of accelerating complexity, the directors who create lasting impact are those who take full ownership of their development. That means choosing the right skills to build, seeking out the most effective learning pathways, and applying those skills to shape the board's response to real-world challenges.

But ownership without structure risks becoming aspiration without traction. The most effective directors turn development intent into a practical roadmap—one aligned with governance needs, board dynamics, and emerging strategic pressures. Here are three core building blocks to help guide that effort:

1. Targeted Skill Commitments

Identify two or three leadership skills you've prioritized. Select pathways—self-directed learning, peer learning, structured education, or expert coaching—that map most naturally to your leadership style and board responsibilities. Focus first on skills that have immediate boardroom relevance, where stronger fluency will accelerate board decision making or stakeholder trust.

2. Governance Calibration Loops

Incorporate regular, trusted feedback mechanisms into your development plan. Whether through board evaluations, peer reflections, or informal chair conversations, create space for recalibration. Governance leadership depends as much on perception and alignment as on technical skill—and calibration ensures development stays strategic, not isolated.

3. Alignment to Governance Priorities

Anchor your leadership growth to where the board is headed. Align skill development to strategic board priorities—whether it's cybersecurity oversight, stakeholder capitalism leadership, or succession planning. Development efforts that align to evolving governance expectations sustain credibility and deepen board impact.

The boards that thrive are led by directors who grow intentionally, adapt visibly, and lead forward through change. Development isn't a separate track. It's woven into leadership credibility itself. And the directors who build with that mindset set the tone for governance that lasts.

As we move into the final case study, we return to David Chen—whose leadership evolution reflects the same themes this chapter has explored. His story isn't a checklist. But it does offer a real-world example of what intentional development looks like when it's built into the rhythm of governance itself—not treated as separate from it.

Evolving Case Study: David Chen Turning Awareness into Action

David Chen didn't need another wake-up call—what he needed was a plan. After the investor meeting that left him rethinking his relevance in the boardroom, he had worked through a prioritization framework to identify the skills that mattered most: technology awareness, to engage confidently in AI oversight; communication, to better navigate high-expectation environments; and authenticity, to show up with clarity and consistency in increasingly complex conversations. Now, the question was how to build those skills—deliberately, not reactively.

He started with self-directed learning. David signed up for an AI-powered education platform designed for corporate directors. The system assessed his baseline knowledge and surfaced short, targeted modules on data governance, predictive analytics, and digital ethics. He supplemented that with governance podcasts and a curated list of AI strategy articles tailored to the boardroom. This helped him move beyond headline-level awareness. He wasn't trying to become an expert—he wanted to ask better questions, understand risks, and participate in conversations that mattered. These efforts deepened his technology awareness in practical, low-friction ways.

Next, he turned to peer learning. David reached out to a fellow director—someone with deep experience in platform governance and stakeholder relations—and proposed a reverse mentorship.

Their conversations, grounded in real-world board dynamics, helped David rethink how he interpreted public sentiment, internal communication challenges, and investor priorities. He began contributing more effectively during discussions about stakeholder positioning—not by dominating, but by listening differently and framing ideas more inclusively. This strengthened his communication skill—particularly in stakeholder-facing scenarios—and began to shape a new kind of presence at the table.

Still, David wanted structure. He enrolled in a short executive education program focused on AI governance and long-term value creation. The program combined formal instruction with interactive simulations on algorithmic bias, digital trust, and emerging regulation. But it was the case study discussions—full of competing priorities and ethical gray zones—that pushed him the most. He had to speak up, take a position, and stay composed under pressure. These moments stretched his ability to lead with authenticity. He didn't have a script—he had to rely on values, clarity, and tone. That skill was harder to build than he expected, but more powerful than he realized.

Finally, he worked with a governance coach to refine how he showed up in real-time board interactions. Together, they focused on narrative clarity—how to shape a point of view without sounding rehearsed. They also practiced adapting his tone depending on audience and context: when to step forward, when to hold space, when to ask instead of advice. These sessions helped him internalize the mindset of a modern director—not just someone who shows up prepared, but someone who shows up ready to lead.

As David committed to the work of development, his boardroom presence began to shift. He didn't feel like a different person—but he was showing up differently. He weighed in with more precision during a discussion on AI-enabled compliance tools. He reframed a tense conversation about public messaging in a way that diffused defensiveness. And when the board was briefed on upcoming ESG disclosures, he asked a series of layered questions that helped clarify both the strategy and the risk posture. He wasn't trying to impress anyone. He was trying to contribute—credibly, constructively, and with intention.

David's journey reinforces a key theme of this book: Knowing what to develop is not enough; taking action is what builds relevance and impact. Through focused effort across all three skill domains, he began to shift not just what he said in the boardroom but how others experienced his leadership. While David engaged across all four development pathways to illustrate what intentional growth can look like in practice, not every board member will take the same route. What matters is choosing the approach that best supports your skill priorities—and following through with intention. His development wasn't finished, but it was finally in motion—by his own design.

Chapter Summary

Today's board members must do more than identify the right leadership skills—they must act with purpose to develop them. With governance responsibilities expanding and disruption accelerating, directors can no longer rely on legacy expertise alone. The most effective board members commit to intentional growth, developing the skills required to lead in moments of uncertainty, complexity, and transformation. This chapter introduced a contemporary approach to board-level development—one that moves beyond passive learning and focuses on deliberate, skill-driven progress.

We explored four distinct pathways for skill building: self-directed learning, peer learning, structured governance education, and expert coaching. Each supports development across the three core domains—professional, personal, and technology—and helps directors strengthen the skills they've prioritized. While these pathways may be used individually or in combination, they all reinforce a simple truth: Relevance in the boardroom is built through continuous, intentional learning. Real-world examples and David Chen's story illustrated how focused development—tailored to the director's role and context—can elevate both confidence and contribution.

With this chapter, we conclude the core content of *The Contemporary Board Member*. In the Conclusion, we will reflect on the leadership themes that have shaped this journey—from evolving board expectations to the emergence of multidimensional governance. The directors who lead effectively in this era will be those who own their development, embrace continuous learning, and bring integrated leadership to the challenges that matter most.

CONCLUSION

Modern Governance Demands Modern Leadership

The Expanding Mandate of Modern Directors

There was a time when board membership was seen as the final step in a leadership career—a capstone built on operational success, industry expertise, and personal reputation. Joining a board signaled arrival. Directors were expected to steward, oversee, and guide—but not necessarily to evolve. Governance was primarily retrospective, focused on accountability for past decisions rather than shaping responses to emerging realities.

That expectation has shifted. Today's directors navigate a governance landscape defined by complexity, transparency, and acceleration. The issues boards must engage—digital disruption, stakeholder capitalism, geopolitical instability, regulatory innovation—move faster than traditional oversight rhythms. Experience alone no longer guarantees readiness. Directors are increasingly evaluated by their ability to lead fluidly across financial, technological, ethical, and societal dimensions—not by past prestige, but by current relevance.

In this environment, boardroom leadership demands more than judgment based on what once worked. It demands active engagement, broader situational awareness, and an integrated leadership approach. Directors who combine strategic clarity with cultural fluency, governance foresight with real-time influence, are the ones who will set the tone for modern governance. The expectations of the seat are greater—and they are constant.

The Contemporary Board Member was built for this evolving reality. It's not about mastering every skill. It's about leading forward—with credibility, adaptability, and the capabilities needed to govern organizations facing unrelenting complexity.

Evolving the Standard for Boardroom Leadership

Across the chapters of *The Contemporary Board Member*, we reframed what effective board leadership now demands. Governance today is no longer about narrow oversight or episodic engagement. It requires directors to operate with influence without direct authority, contribute without ego, and engage strategically across a much broader range of leadership dimensions.

To support this evolution, we reintroduced the three leadership domains first explored in *The Contemporary Leader*—professional, personal, and technology skills—and adapted them to the realities of modern boardroom dynamics. Within those domains, we revisited the 15 essential leadership skills that now form the bedrock of credible governance.

But skills alone are not the endpoint. They are the starting line. As explored throughout the book, it is the thoughtful combination and application of these skills that transforms them into leadership competencies—competencies that enable directors to respond credibly to forces like AI disruption, stakeholder activism, regulatory acceleration, and geopolitical volatility.

This is the model we've offered: Skills are the foundation. Competencies are the differentiators. And leadership impact at the board level depends on how effectively directors activate these competencies across the shifting forces of governance today. Simple in structure. Transformational in practice.

Prioritization Is Strategic, Not Optional

Not every board member will build the same skills in the same way. That's not the goal. What matters is intentionality. In Chapter 3, we introduced a practical framework to help directors identify where to focus their development based on five key factors—role, organizational context, peer dynamics, personal growth edge, and long-term governance trends.

This was not a prescriptive formula. It was a permission structure—a way to move beyond assumptions or checklists and instead approach leadership growth with strategic focus. Because in a governance environment with this dynamic, the real risk is not falling short of perfection—it's failing to adapt at all.

The directors who will have the greatest impact are those who can step back, reassess their leadership range, and prioritize what their board needs next—not just what they've delivered before.

Action Converts Insight into Impact

In Chapter 4, we explored how board members can move from insight to action. Through four clear development pathways—self-directed learning, peer learning, structured education, and expert coaching—we showed how board members can build the specific skills they've prioritized in ways that are both personalized and practical.

These learning strategies are not just developmental—they are governance tools. They help directors stay current, deepen their contributions, and shape boardroom culture in ways that align with today's external pressures. Importantly, they reinforce a mindset we've returned to throughout this book: Leadership at the board level is not episodic. It is practiced. It is developed. It is earned—again and again.

Whether refining communication in stakeholder-facing moments, developing AI fluency, or building adaptability, what matters most is progress—the kind that's anchored in skill, not just experience.

Leadership Is a Continuous Decision

At its core, *The Contemporary Board Member* is a book about decisions—not just the ones directors help organizations make, but the ones they must make about their own leadership. The decision to evolve. To learn. To stay in motion, even when experience might offer the temptation to stand still.

Because in today's governance landscape, tenure isn't a substitute for readiness. And credentials aren't a proxy for range. The most effective directors are those who treat leadership not as an achievement, but as an ongoing responsibility.

There is no arrival point. There is only the next meeting. The next challenge. The next moment where clarity, courage, and competency are needed.

A Series. A Standard. A Signal.

This book is part of a broader conversation—a continuation of the leadership journey begun in *The Contemporary Leader*. While the contexts may differ, the foundation remains the same: In a world defined by uncertainty, organizations need leaders who are not just experienced but evolving. Leaders who understand that governance today demands not only oversight but contribution. Not only experience but readiness.

To be a contemporary board member is to reject stagnation. It is to engage fully with the complexity that governance now demands—financial, technological, ethical, and societal. It is to believe that while none of us will master every skill, we each have a responsibility—to our boards, our organizations, and ourselves—to build the capabilities that unlock our greatest contribution.

This volume is part of *The Contemporary Leader* series—alongside *The Contemporary Executive* and *The Contemporary Entrepreneur*. Each explores a different leadership context. Each reinforces a simple truth: Modern leadership effectiveness is built on skill, shaped by context, and refined with intention.

You won't find a checklist at the end of this book. That's by design. The journey of boardroom leadership is not linear. It is situational. It is iterative. And above all, it is deeply human.

So take stock of where you are. Reflect on where your leadership is strong—and where it needs to stretch. Lean into the tools, frameworks, and ideas shared here. Not with pressure to perfect, but with the conviction to grow and extend your impact.

Because while governance evolves with the world around us, leadership evolves by choice. And that choice is yours.

ABOUT THE AUTHOR

For over three decades, Tom Mawhinney has navigated the ever-evolving business landscape as a board member, senior executive, consultant, and entrepreneur. His career has spanned industries, continents, and economic cycles—each experience reinforcing a fundamental truth: leadership is the catalyst for organizational success.

A recognized expert in contemporary leadership, strategic growth, and emerging technologies, Tom has helped businesses worldwide evolve, adapt, and thrive in an era of rapid transformation. His ability to bridge the gap between traditional leadership principles and the disruptive forces of AI, digital transformation, and shifting workforce dynamics has made him a sought-after advisor to executives and board members alike.

Driven by an insatiable curiosity and a commitment to continuous learning, Tom remains at the forefront of leadership evolution. His thought leadership, built on years of hands-on experience and keen market insight, offers a pragmatic approach to navigating the complexities of modern business. In his writing, speaking, and advisory roles, he empowers leaders to embrace change, unlock potential, and drive sustained growth in an unpredictable world.

Email: Tom@TheContemporaryLeader.com

Website: www.TheContemporaryLeader.com

LinkedIn: https://www.linkedin.com/in/tommawhinney

THE CONTEMPORARY LEADER SERIES

The Contemporary Leader Series is a modern leadership collection designed for today's rapidly evolving business landscape. Based on the foundational framework introduced in The Contemporary Leader, each book delivers role-specific insights tailored to the unique demands of board members, executives, and entrepreneurs.

Whether you're guiding strategy from the boardroom, driving performance as a senior executive, or building the future as a founder, this series helps you translate essential leadership skills into practical impact. With a focus on professional, personal, and technology domains, each volume equips you to lead with agility, foresight, and purpose in an era of constant change.

The Contemporary Leader

The foundational leadership guide for navigating today's fast-changing business environment across all leadership contexts.

The Contemporary Board Member

A practical approach to governing with strategic clarity, long-range insight, and confidence in complexity.

The Contemporary Executive

Equipping operational leaders with the skills to lead teams, drive results, and adapt to ongoing transformation.

The Contemporary Entrepreneur

Designed for builders and founders scaling with speed, purpose, and modern leadership capability.

www.TheContemporaryLeader.com

DID YOU ENJOY THIS BOOK?

If you enjoyed reading this book, you can help by suggesting it to someone else you think might like it, and **please leave a positive review** wherever you purchased it. This does a lot in helping others find the book. We thank you in advance for taking a few moments to do this.

THANK YOU

You might also like other Thin Leaf Press titles:

The AI Mindset: Thriving Within Civilization's Next Big Disruption

AI: Work Smarter and Live Better Within Civilization's Next Big Disruption

Peak Performance: Mindset Tools for Managers

Peak Performance: Mindset Tools for Sales

Peak Performance: Mindset Tools for Leaders

Peak Performance: Mindset Tools for Business

Peak Performance: Mindset Tools for Entrepreneurs

Peak Performance: Mindset Tools for Athletes

The Successful Mind: Tools to Living a Purposeful, Productive, and Happy Life

The Successful Body: Using Fitness, Nutrition, and Mindset to Live Better

The Successful Spirit: Top Performers Share Secrets to a Winning Mindset

Winning Mindset: Elite Strategies for Peak Performance

Winner's Mindset: Peak Performance Strategies for Success

The Life Coach's Tool Kit, Vol. 1

The Life Coach's Tool Kit, Vol. 2

The Life Coach's Tool Kit, Vol. 3

Ordinary to Extraordinary

The Magical Lightness of Being

Explore.

NOTES

NOTES

NOTES

NOTES

NOTES

NOTES

NOTES

NOTES

NOTES

NOTES

www.ingramcontent.com/pod-product-compliance
Lightning Source LLC
Chambersburg PA
CBHW071537120626
46550CB00006B/2486